THE CHARLIE BROWN COLLECTION™

CONTENTS

ISBN 978-1-4950-5165-4

HAL•LEONARD®
CORPORATION
7777 W. BLUEMOUND RD. P.O. BOX 13819 MILWAUKEE, WI 53213

PEANUTS © United Feature Syndicate, Inc.
www.snoopy.com

In Australia Contact:
Hal Leonard Australia Pty. Ltd.
4 Lentara Court
Cheltenham, Victoria, 3192 Australia
Email: ausadmin@halleonard.com.au

Visit Hal Leonard Online at
www.halleonard.com

BLUE CHARLIE BROWN

By VINCE GUARALDI

Moderate Swing

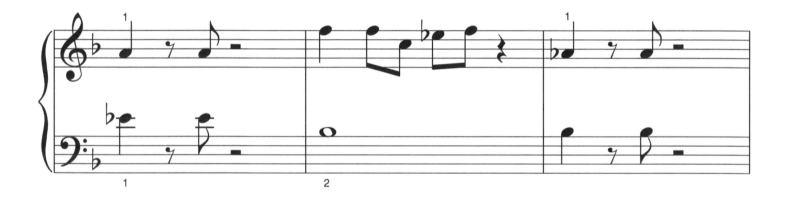

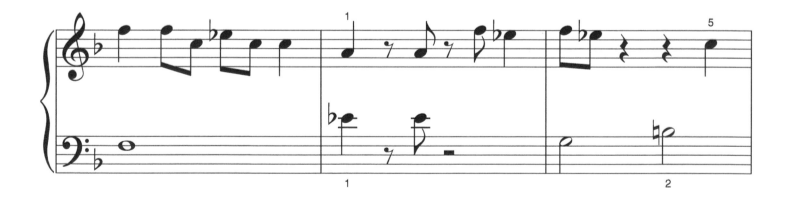

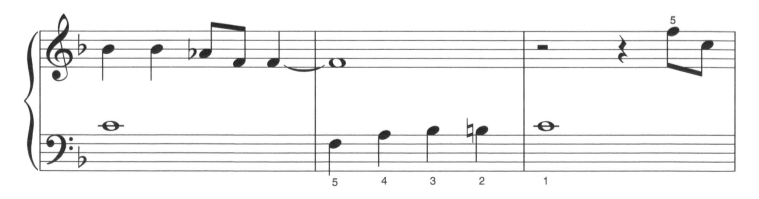

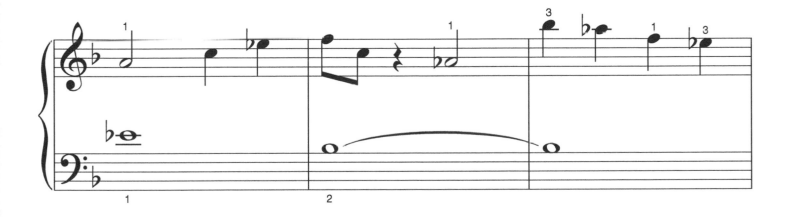
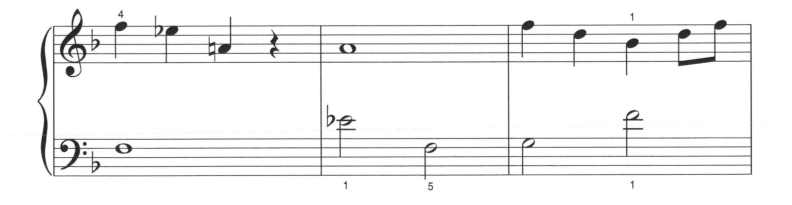
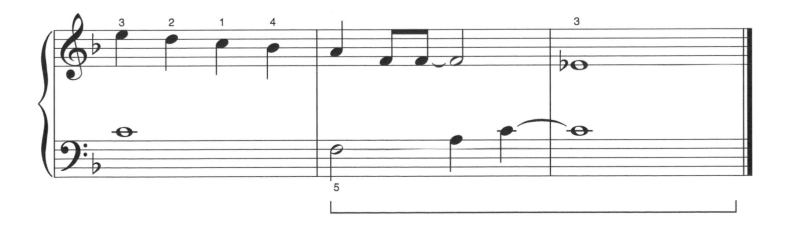

CHARLIE BROWN THEME

By VINCE GUARALDI

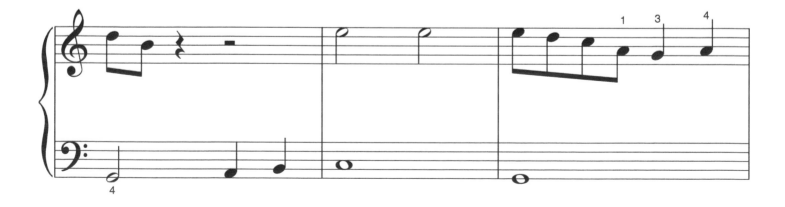

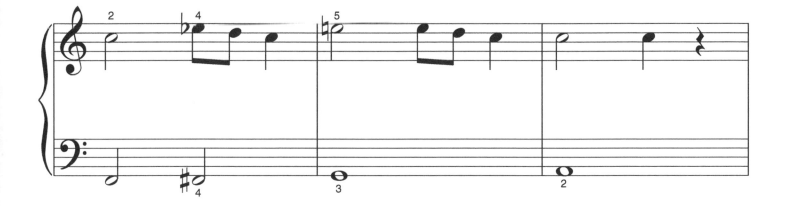

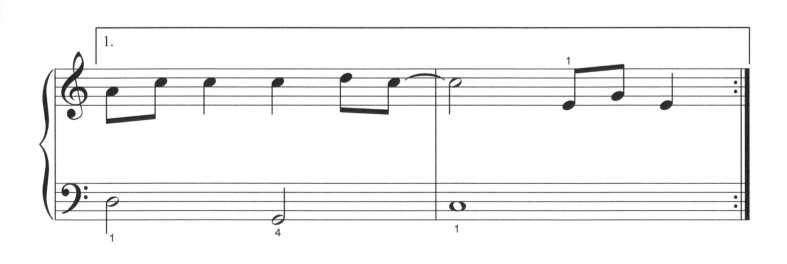

LOVE WILL COME

By VINCE GUARALDI

Moderately, with feeling

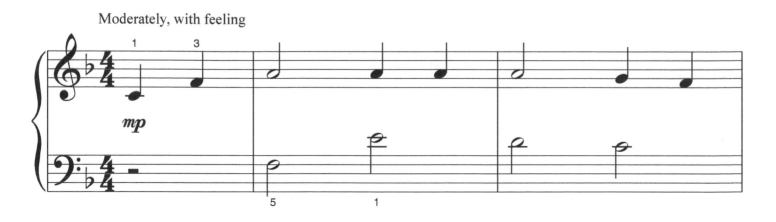

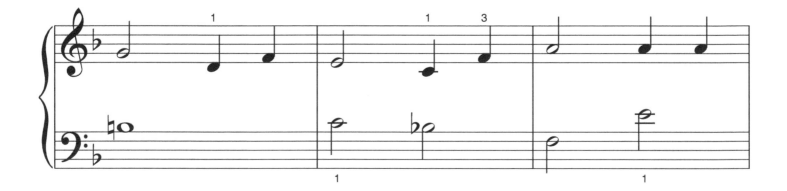

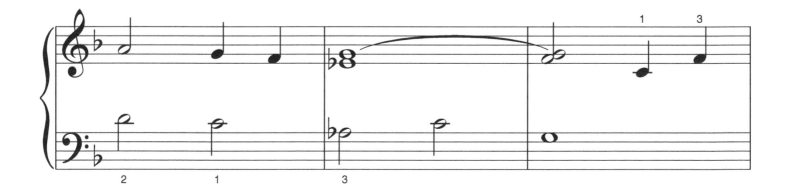

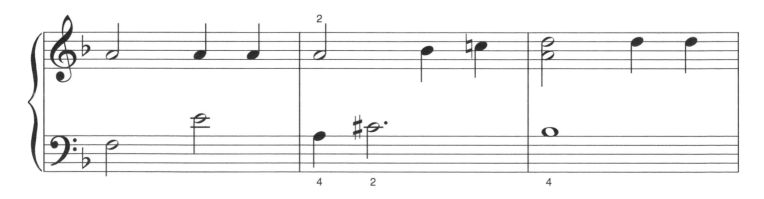

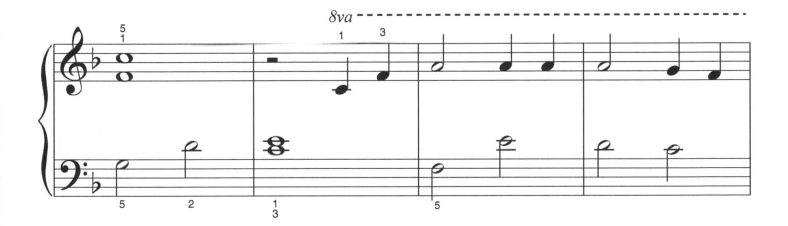
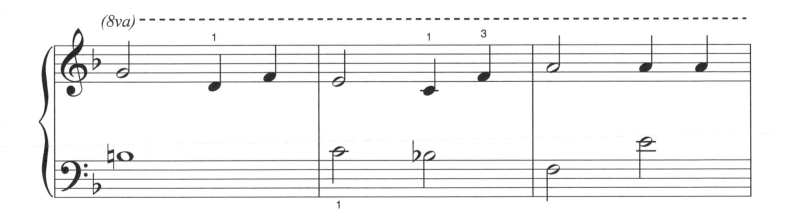
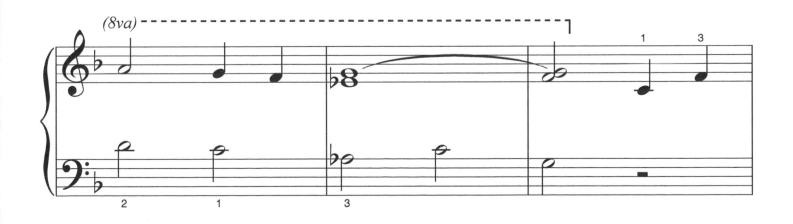

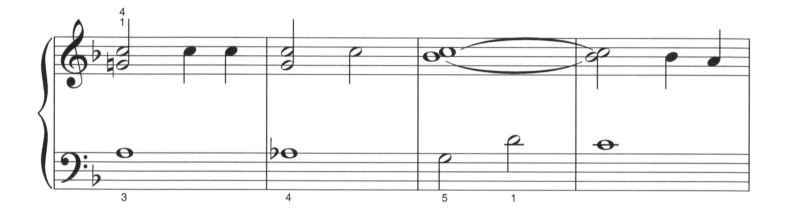

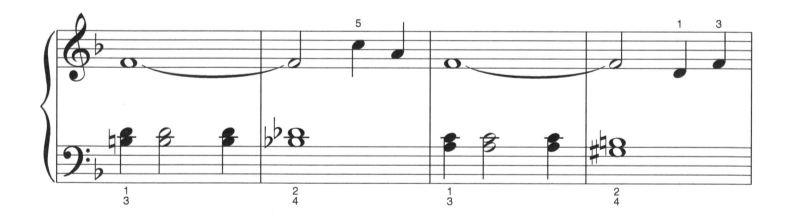

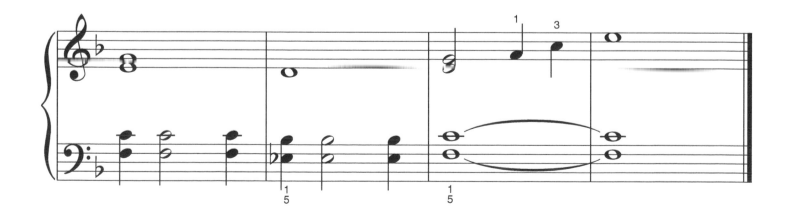

CHRISTMAS IS COMING

from A CHARLIE BROWN CHRISTMAS

By VINCE GUARALDI

Rock Bossa Nova

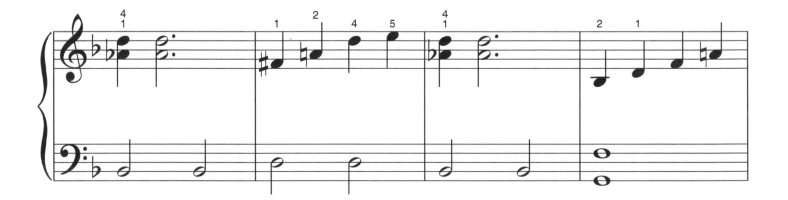

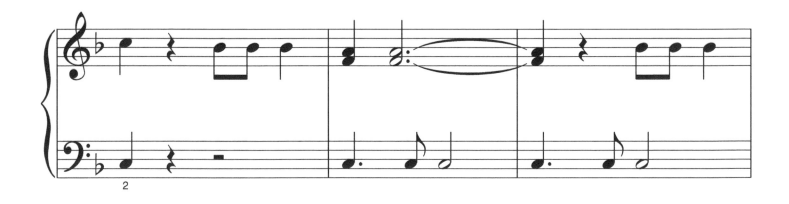

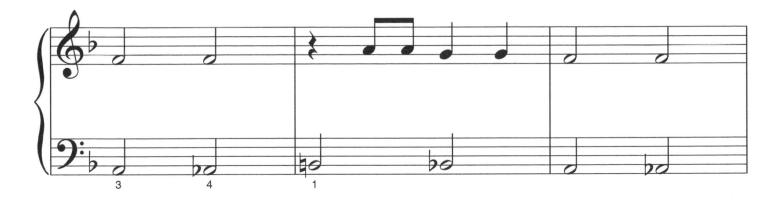

CHRISTMAS TIME IS HERE

from A CHARLIE BROWN CHRISTMAS

Words by LEE MENDELSON
Music by VINCE GUARALDI

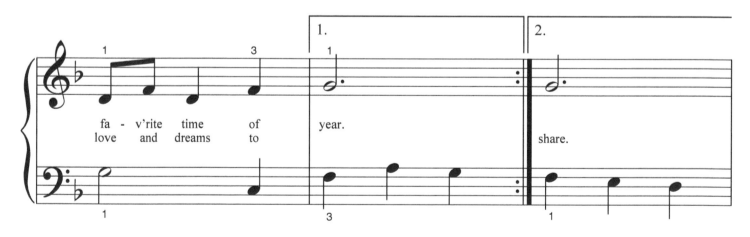

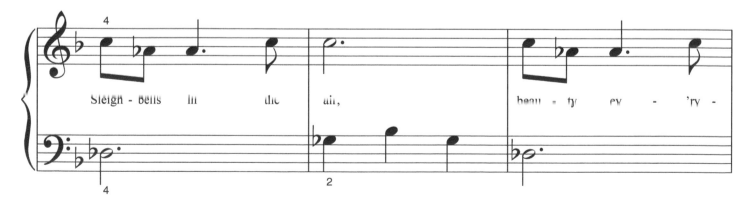

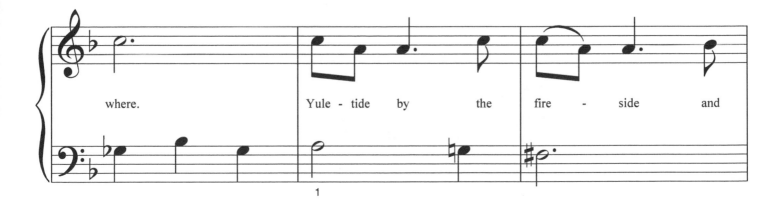

where. Yule - tide by the fire - side and

joy - ful mem - 'ries there. Christ-mas time is here,

we'll be draw - ing near. Oh, that we could

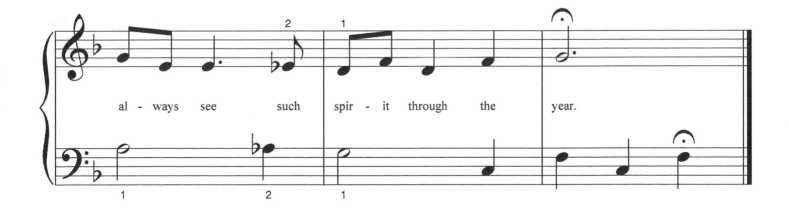

al - ways see such spir - it through the year.

PEPPERMINT PATTY

By VINCE GUARALDI

Moderately

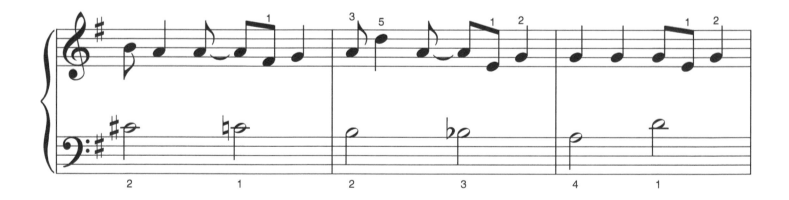

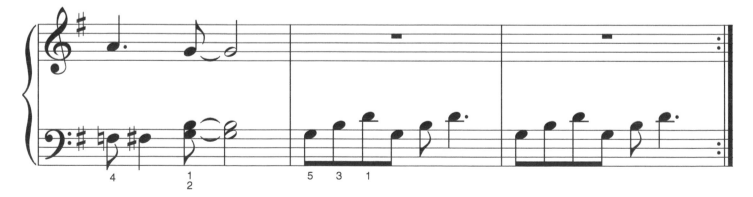

THE GREAT PUMPKIN WALTZ

By VINCE GUARALDI

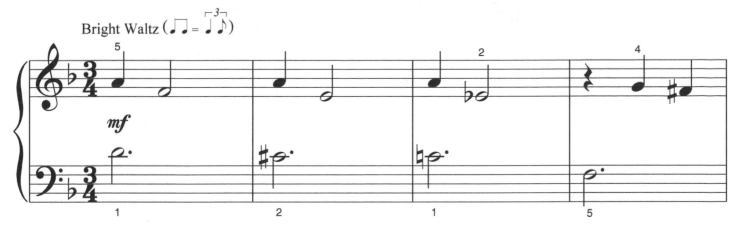

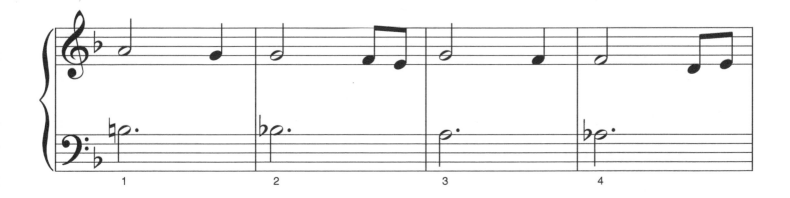

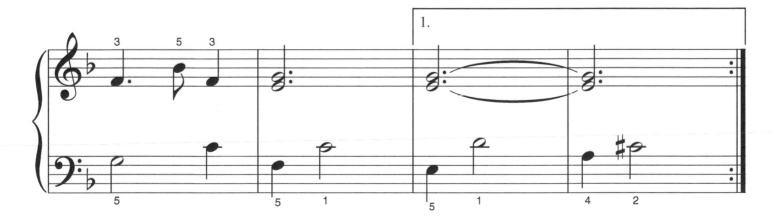

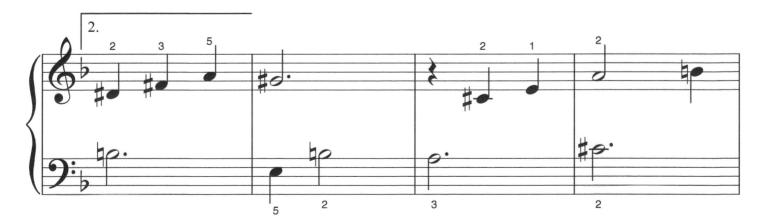

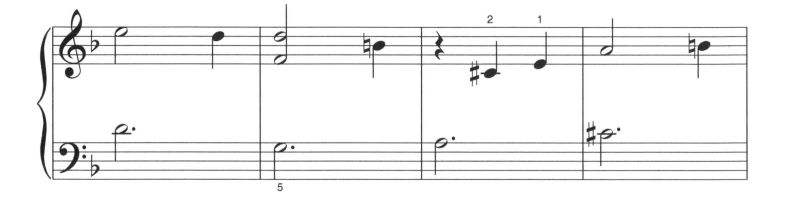

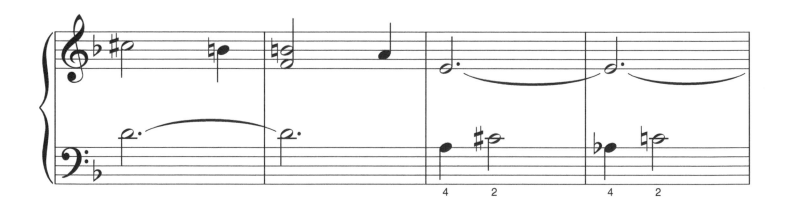

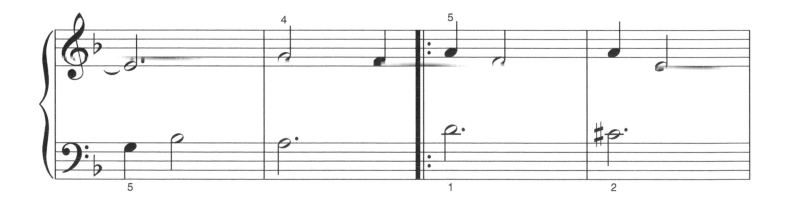

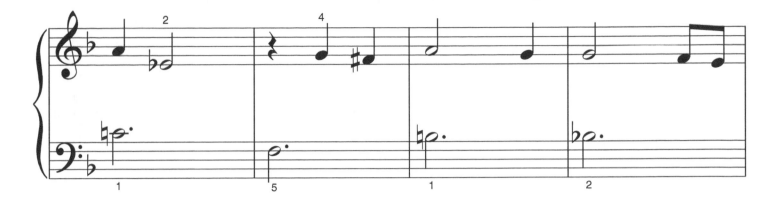

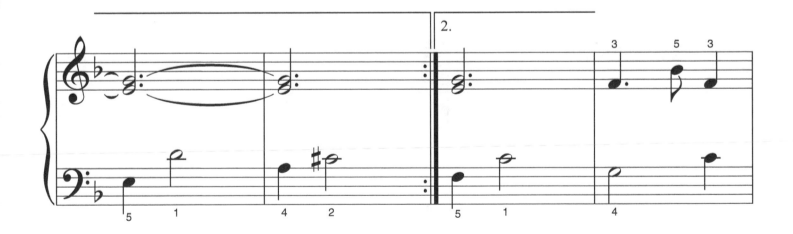

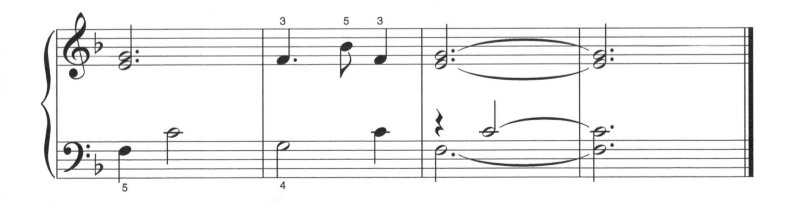

HAPPINESS THEME

By VINCE GUARALDI

Easy Jazz Waltz

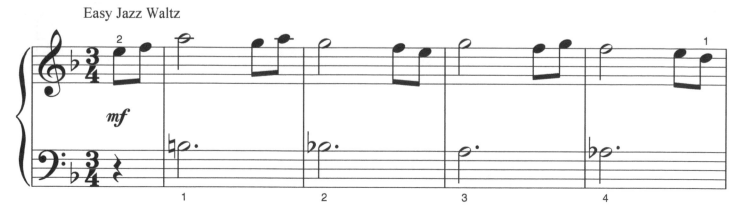

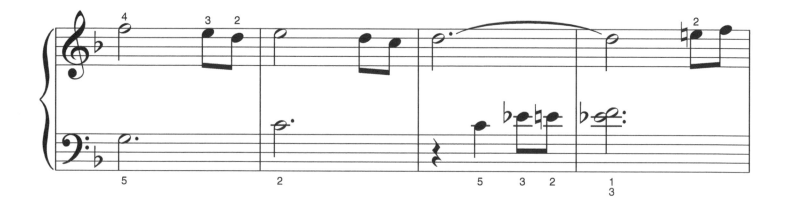

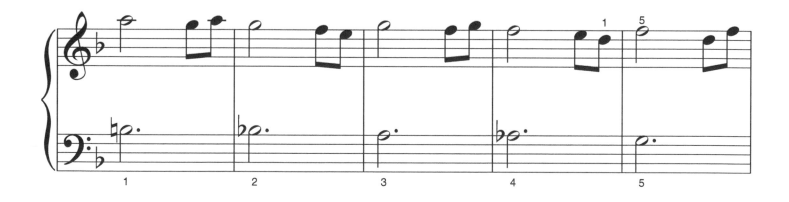

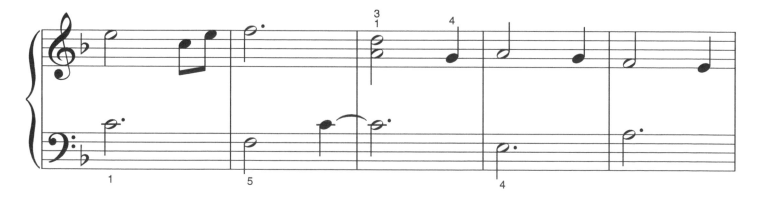

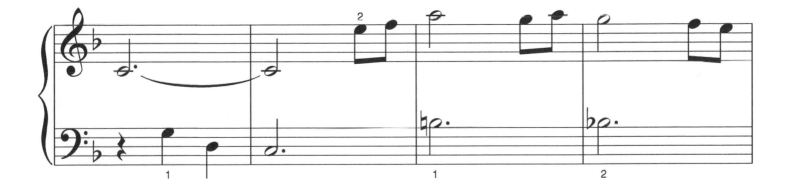

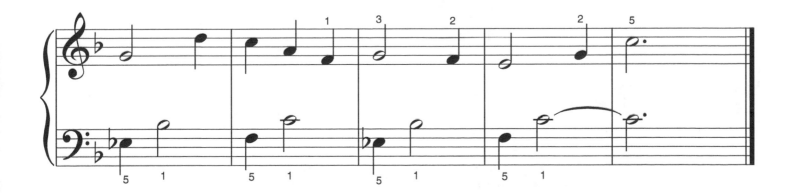

LINUS AND LUCY

By VINCE GUARALDI

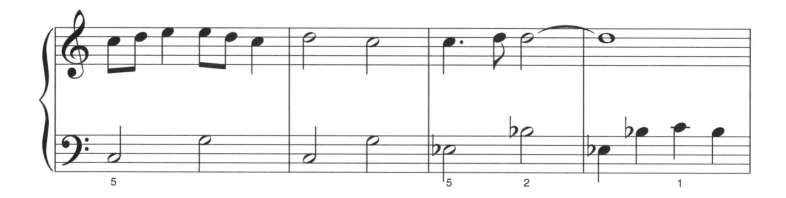

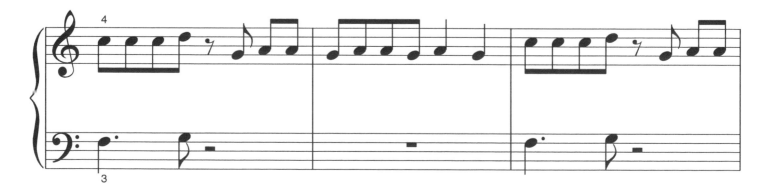

SKATING

By VINCE GUARALDI

Bright Jazz Waltz

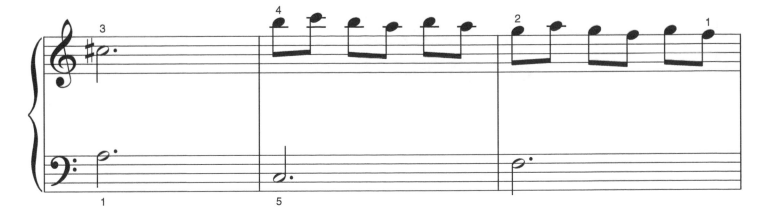

To Coda ⊕

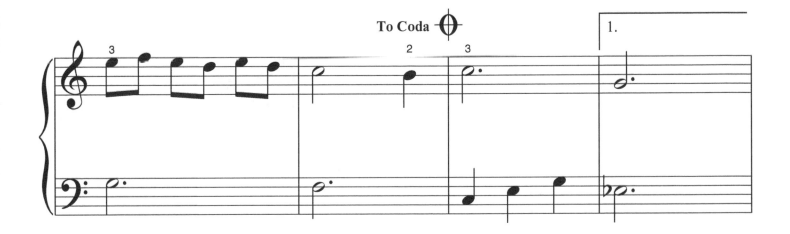

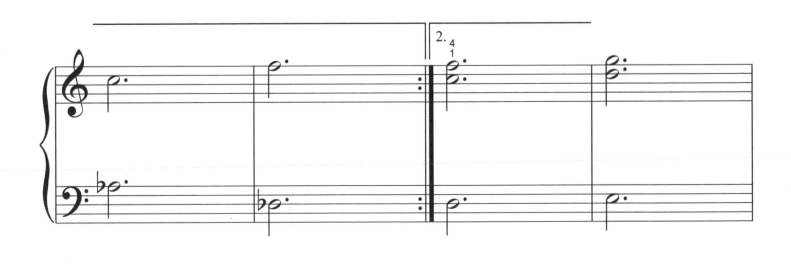

25

D.S. al Coda

CODA

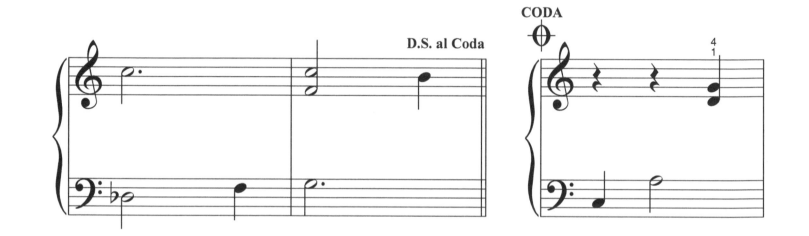

rit.

RED BARON

By VINCE GUARALDI

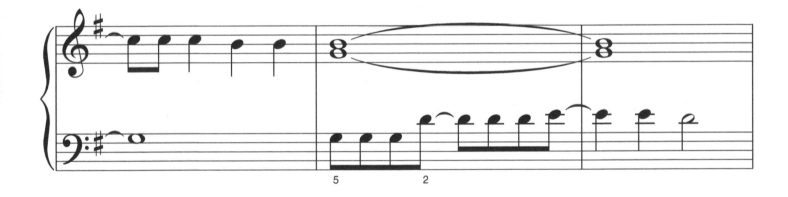

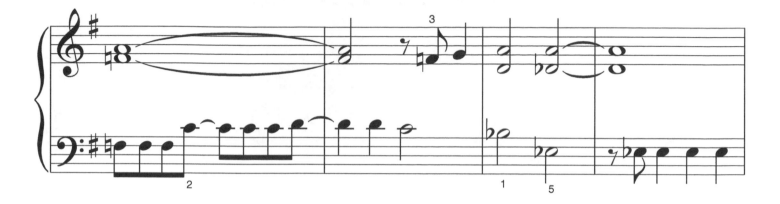

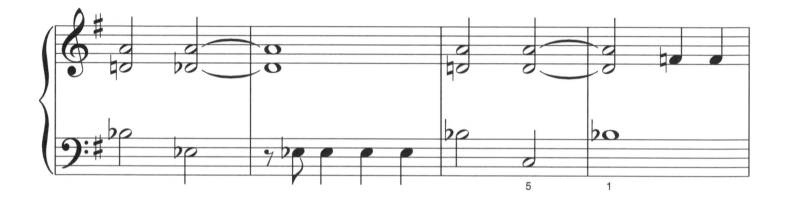

To Coda ⊕

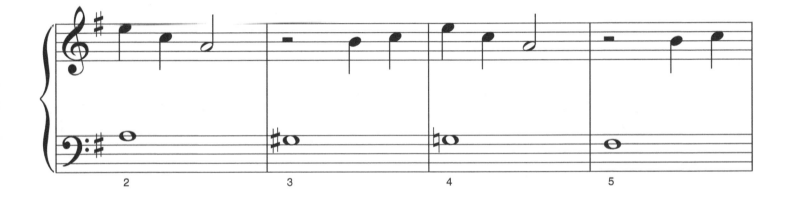

D.S. al Coda

CODA

YOU'RE IN LOVE, CHARLIE BROWN

By VINCE GUARALDI

Bright Waltz

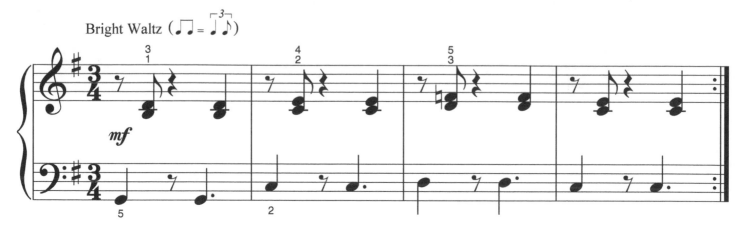

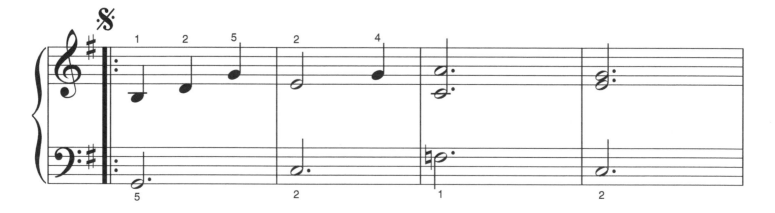

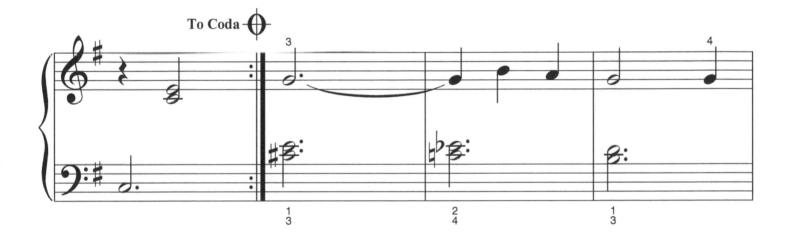

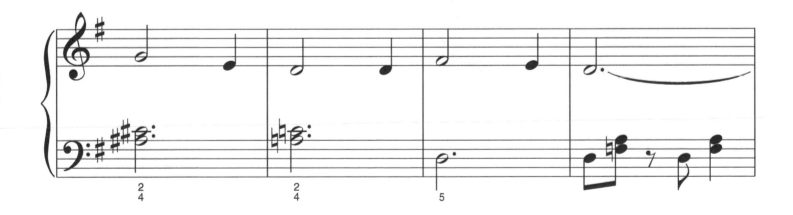

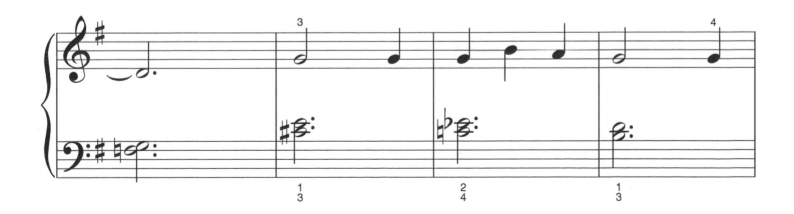

32

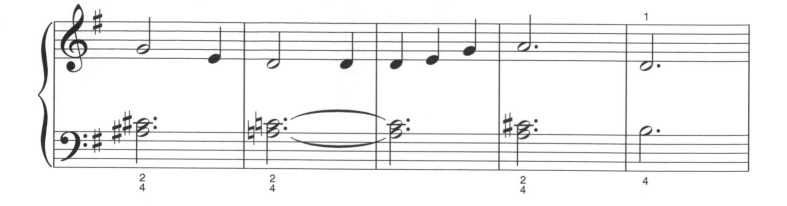

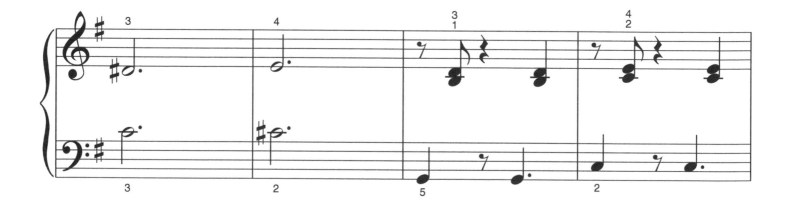

D.S. al Coda
(no repeat)

CODA

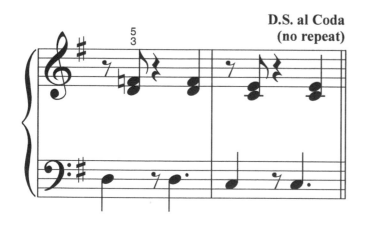

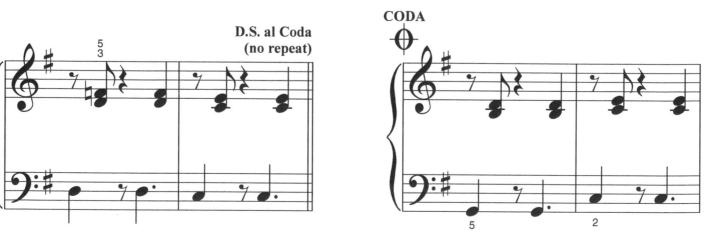